I WANT TO KNOW...

What buildings
do people call home?

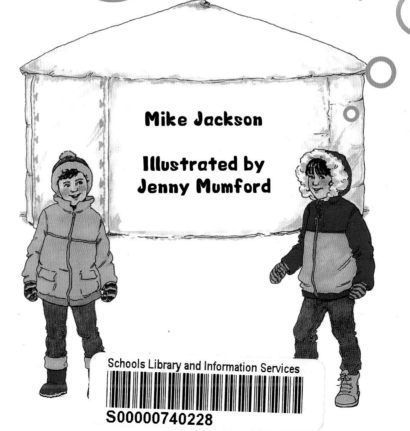

Mike Jackson

Illustrated by
Jenny Mumford

First published in this edition in 2011 by
Evans Publishing Group
2A Portman Mansions
Chiltern Street
London W1U 6NR

© Evans Brothers Limited 2011

www.evansbooks.co.uk

British Library Cataloguing in Publication Data:
A CIP catalogue record for this book is available from the British Library

ISBN: 9780237544881

Planned and produced by Discovery Books
Cover designed by Rebecca Fox

For permission to reproduce copyright material the author and publishers gratefully
acknowledge the following: Bryan and Cherry Alexander: page 26; Ancient Art and Architecture
Collections: page 16; Image Bank: page 18; istock: cover; Spectrum: page 22; Tony Stone: pages 6,
10, 12, 14, 20, 24; Zefa: page 8.

Printed by Great Wall Printing Company in Chai Wan, Hong Kong,
August 2011, Job Number 1672.

CONTENTS

People around the world live in
many different kinds of houses.

Let's go and see some of
them in the magic helicopter!

We have landed
near to the
North Pole,
in Canada.

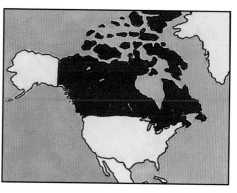

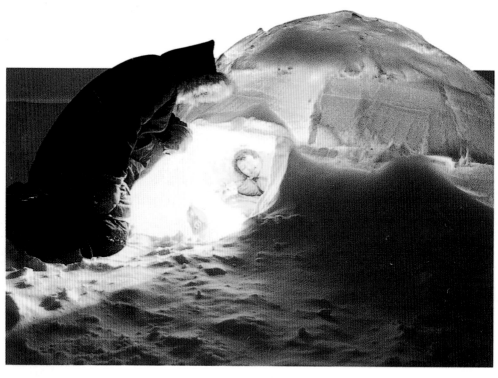

People here sometimes build
shelters out of blocks of ice.
The shelters are called igloos.

6

The Inuit build igloos to sleep in when they go hunting.

It looks cold but it's really warm and snug inside.

Our next stop is the American Southwest. The Pueblo Indians live here.

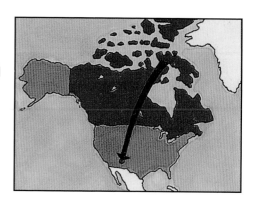

They live in flat-roofed adobe houses.

Adobe are clay bricks that have been dried in the sun.

Now we are
in Zimbabwe,
a country
in Africa.

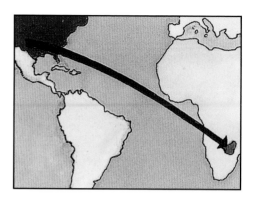

Some farming people in Africa live in round mud huts.

How do they build the huts?

They make a frame of poles and cover it with mud and straw. They use tall elephant grass for the roof.

Now let's go to Morocco, in North Africa. The houses have flat roofs because there is very little rain.

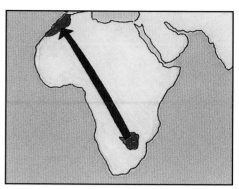

These houses stay very cool
inside because the walls
are thick and the windows
are small.

Goodbye Africa, hello Europe! Now we are in the Alps in Switzerland.

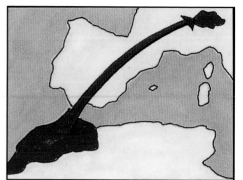

Many people here live in chalets with gently sloping roofs.

The snow stays on the roof and keeps the house warm.

Welcome to France! Many thousands of years ago people lived in these caves.

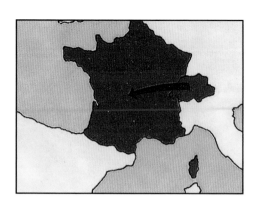

They painted pictures on the cave walls.

Our next stop
is in Ireland.
Caravans like
this one used
to be homes
for Travellers.

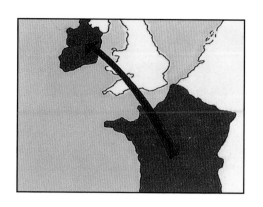

They were pulled by horses.

This cottage
in England
was built over
400 years ago.
It has a
thatched roof.

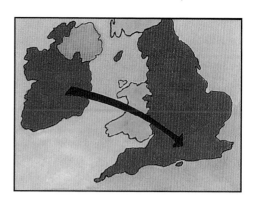

Thatch is made from straw or
water reeds.

21

Just over 4,000 miles away, we land in Mongolia. Those large round tents are called yurts.

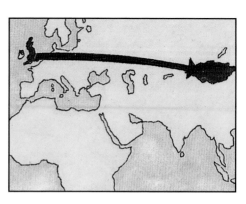

The people who live in these yurts are nomads. They can take their tents with them as they move from place to place.

Yurts are made from layers of felt made out of sheep's wool.

Let's travel
further east
to Japan.

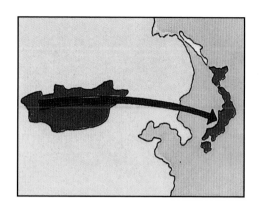

In this traditional Japanese
house, the rooms are divided by
sliding doors made out of paper.

25

Welcome to
Hong Kong
harbour.
Some people in
Hong Kong live
on boats like
this one.

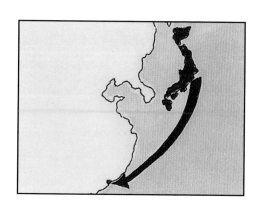

The people who live on the boats are fishermen.

The fishermen sell their catch to restaurants and markets.

Fun activities

Here are some of the houses that the children saw on their journey. Can you match each picture to the correct place in the list below? Can you remember what they are each called?

Hong Kong   England
Zimbabwe   Canada
Mongolia   Switzerland

Draw your own cave painting like the one you can see on page 16.

Have a look at some cave paintings on the Internet to help you. Will you include large wild animals, like bison or horses, or even woolly mammoths? Will you show people in your painting?

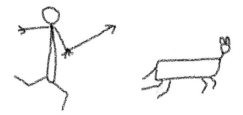

What would your imaginary house be like?

Would it be round or square, or another shape entirely? What would the walls and roof be made of? Would it be tall and thin, or short and wide? Would it be underground, or even underwater? Write a story describing your ideal house.

Interesting websites:

Build your own home at:
http://www.bbc.co.uk/scotland/education/wwww/homes/kids/index_choice.shtml

Find out about more houses round the world:
http://www.hgpho.to/wfest/house/house-e.html

Learn about houses and homes through history:
http://www.woodlands-junior.kent.sch.uk/homework/houses.html

Index